FIFE EDUCATION
COMMITTEE

KING'S ROAD P. SCHOOL
ROSYTH

TASTE

Wayne Jackman

Reading consultant:
Diana Bentley
University of Reading

Photographs by
Chris Fairclough

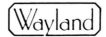

The Senses

Touch
Sight
Hearing
Smell
Taste

Editor: Janet De Saulles

First published in 1989 by
Wayland (Publishers) Ltd
61 Western Road, Hove
East Sussex, BN3 1JD, England

British Library Cataloguing in Publication Data
Jackman, Wayne
   Taste.
   1.Man. Taste. For children
   I. Title   II. Fairclough, Chris   III. Series
   612'.87

   ISBN 1–85210–733–2

Phototypeset by Kalligraphics Ltd, Horley, Surrey, England
Printed and bound by Casterman S.A., Belgium

Contents

All the words that appear
in **bold** are explained in the
glossary on page 22.

Tastes good enough to eat.

There are five **senses** – sight, touch, smell, hearing and taste. This book is about taste. You use your tongue to taste things. As our sense of taste is not very strong it likes to work with a partner, smell. If food smells good then it usually tastes good too. Can you remember what the things in the photo below taste like?

Why do we need our sense of taste?

Our senses often protect us from harm. But our sense of taste does not always do this. Sometimes even when food has gone bad it does not taste odd. So we might still eat it and become ill. Even though our taste sense does not always notice danger, we would not want to be without it. How dull all our food would be if we could not enjoy the lovely tastes.

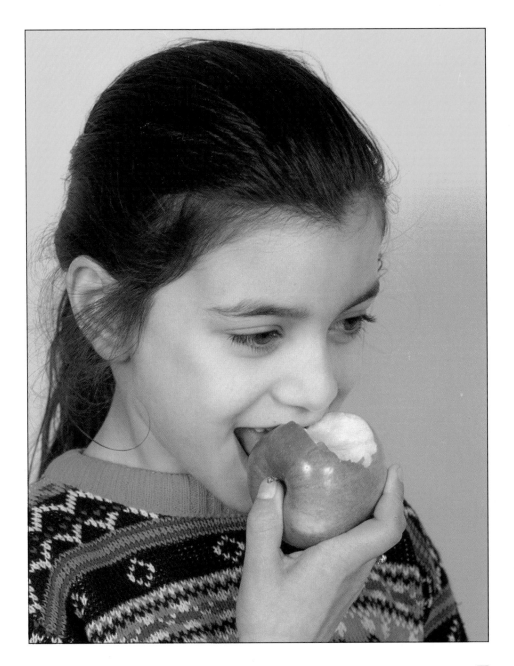

Sweet or sour?

We can taste lots of different flavours in our food, but they are all either sour, sweet, salty or bitter. A melon is sweet. What else is? Milk chocolate is sweet, but plain (dark) chocolate is bitter. Sometimes grown-ups prefer plain chocolate. Crisps often have a salty flavour, and lemons have a sour taste. Try to think of some other foods and their tastes. Which one is your favourite?

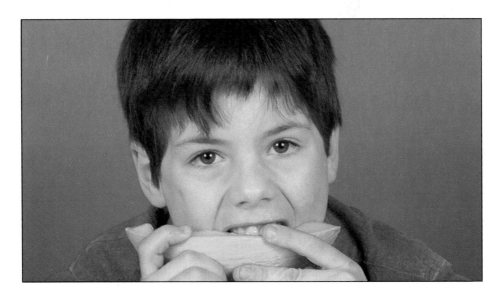

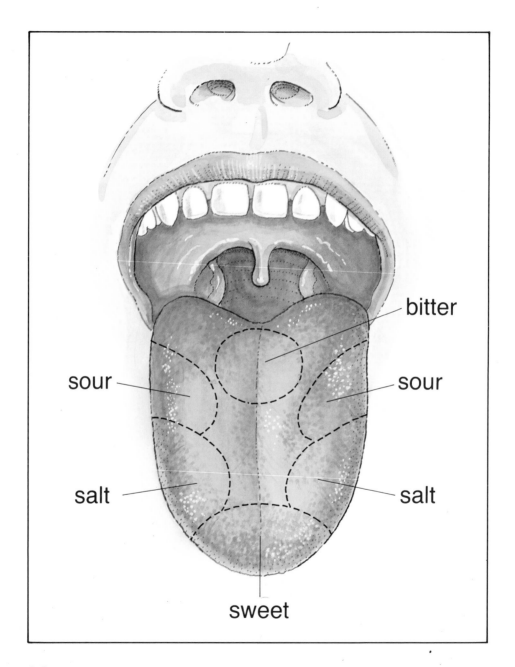

bitter

sour

sour

salt

salt

sweet

How do I taste things?

Look at the picture opposite. Your tongue is covered with little spots called **taste buds**. Some taste buds can recognize one taste better than others. Can you see which part is good at tasting sweet things? The sides taste the salty or sour things. The back tastes bitter things. Most foods are a mixture of tastes. The children in the photo below are eating food with many different flavours.

I cannot taste a thing.

Sometimes our taste buds are lazy. When we have a bad cold our food does not taste very good. This is because our sense of smell helps us to taste things. If you cannot smell something you can hardly taste it either. Our taste buds also stop working for a while if we eat something cold, like an ice lolly.

Dry food is difficult to taste.

Dry things, such as cream crackers, are difficult to taste or swallow. When we eat food we need to mix it with the water our mouth makes. We often call this water spit but its proper name is **saliva**. It carries the food's flavour to the bottom of the taste buds. It also makes the food into a smooth paste which is easy to swallow. The boy in the picture below is getting ready to enjoy his meal.

Things to do.

1. Blindfold one, or perhaps two friends and ask them to pinch their noses shut so that they cannot smell. Offer them a piece of apple and a piece of raw potato. Can they tell the difference?

2. Put some water into four glasses. Add some honey to the first, salt to the second, lemon juice to the third, and coffee to the last glass. Sip each one in turn and swish it round your mouth. Which part of your tongue tastes it? Between each different test clean your tongue with water or bread.

Another experiment.

Our eyes help us to recognize the food we are eating and to know what taste to expect. Make sure that there is an adult near you when you play this game. Get a potato, a swede, a turnip, an apple, a banana and a pear. Peel them and cut a square out of each one. They will all look the same. Ask a friend to taste them and guess what they are.

19

One last look.

Ask a friend to stick out his or her tongue.
Now examine it with a strong **magnifying
glass**. Can you see the tiny taste buds? Like
other parts of the body, people's tongues
have many different sizes and shapes.
Whatever your tongue's shape, its taste buds
will help you to enjoy all the lovely flavours
of food.

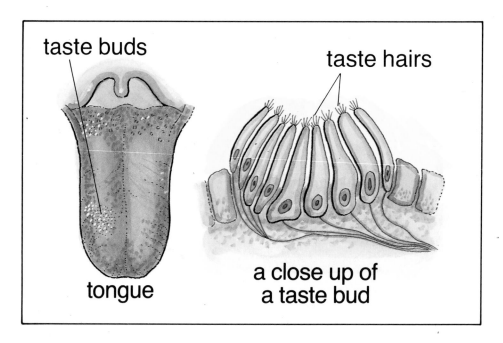

taste buds

taste hairs

tongue

a close up of
a taste bud

Glossary

Magnifying glass   This is made of a special rounded piece of glass. It makes things look as if they are bigger.

Saliva   This is the liquid the mouth makes. It helps us to taste our food and to swallow it.

Senses   We use our senses to know what things look, feel, smell, sound and taste like.

Taste buds   These are the little white spots on our tongues which let us taste food.

Books to read

I Taste With My Tongue by Joan Mills
(Schofield & Son, 1986)
Tasting by Henry Pluckrose (Franklin
Watts, 1985)
Touch, Taste and Smell by Brian Ward
(Franklin Watts, 1982)
Your Senses by D. Baldwin & C. Lister
(Wayland, 1983)

Acknowledgements

The author and Publisher would like to thank the Headteachers, staff and pupils of Millfield Junior School, Elmcroft Street, London, and St Bernadette's School, Atkins Road, Clapham Park, London, for their help in producing this book.

Index